Editorial Project Manager
Lorin E. Klistoff, M.A.

Managing Editor
Karen Goldfluss, M.S. Ed.

Illustrator
Tracy Reynolds

Cover Artist
Barb Lorseyedi

Art Manager
Kevin Barnes

Art Director
CJae Froshay

Imaging
James Edward Grace
Craig Gunnell

Publisher
Mary D. Smith, M.S. Ed.

PHONICS WORD SORTS

GRADES 2-3

sh

fishing

fashion

/sh/spelled sh

cushion

Author

Jeanne Baca Schulte, M.A.

Teacher Created Resources

Teacher Created Resources, Inc.
6421 Industry Way
Westminster, CA 92683
www.teachercreated.com

ISBN-1-4206-3124-1

©2005 Teacher Created Resources, Inc.
Made in U.S.A.

Table of Contents

Introduction

Full-Color Word Sorts supports research that shows word-sorting activities are an exceptional way for students to make connections between words, sounds, and spelling patterns thereby increasing their knowledge of phonological awareness, phoneme awareness, grapheme understanding, and the alphabetic principle.

Full-Color Word Sorts is based on developmental spelling research indicating that students gain word knowledge in the following order:

- letter/sound correspondences
- long/short vowel pattern associations
- syllable and affix structures
- derivational stem/root families

The categories in this book include commonly confused word endings with multiple syllables, silent letters, same spelling–different sounds, and same sound–different spelling sorts. Each sort is organized within the section from easiest to most challenging.

The sorting activities are easily integrated into whole class, small group, or individual center assignments.

In a whole-group setting, teachers introduce the sorting patterns by posting each chart page on the wall. The word cards accompanying the sort are passed out to the students, or copies of the word cards are made for each student. The teacher writes each word on the board/overhead and says it aloud. Students hold up the correct word from their piles, or the student with that word posts it on the correct chart. Students take turns posting the words until the list is complete. (*Note:* Some charts illustrate one answer to help students start the sort.)

In a small-group setting, the teacher will give the word pattern list to the entire class ahead of time. Students turn the cards over one at a time, say the word on the card, spell the word on the card, and place the card on the correct side, or all cards are dealt to the group and students take turns saying and placing each card. Teachers can choose to have students complete the fill-in page included with each sort as a quick way to identify those students needing additional instruction.

In an individual setting, a student can complete the activity on his or her own, or a teacher can choose to use the sort as an evaluation tool to determine the needs of each child. An assessment page (page 4) is included in this book to help teachers keep track of student progress.

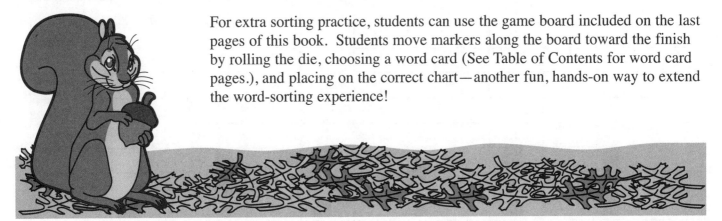

For extra sorting practice, students can use the game board included on the last pages of this book. Students move markers along the board toward the finish by rolling the die, choosing a word card (See Table of Contents for word card pages.), and placing on the correct chart—another fun, hands-on way to extend the word-sorting experience!

Assessment Record

STUDENTS	-CH/-TCH/-GE/-DGE	-LD/-ND	-EL/-LE/-AL/-LL	-AR/-OR/-ER/-URE	-AN/-AIN/-EN/-EON/-ON/-IN	KN/N/WR/R	PH/F/-M/-MB	SILENT B/G/H/L/T/W	Y = LONG E/Y = LONG I	SOUNDS OF SHORT A	SOUNDS OF OU	SOUNDS OF CH	SOUNDS OF OUGH	SPELLING OF LONG A	SPELLING OF LONG E	SPELLING OF /AIR/	SPELLING OF /AW/AWL/	SPELLING OF /EAR/	SPELLING OF /OR/	SPELLING OF /SH/	SPELLING OF /OO/

-ch words

bench

-tch words

ditch

-ge words

large

-dge words

bridge

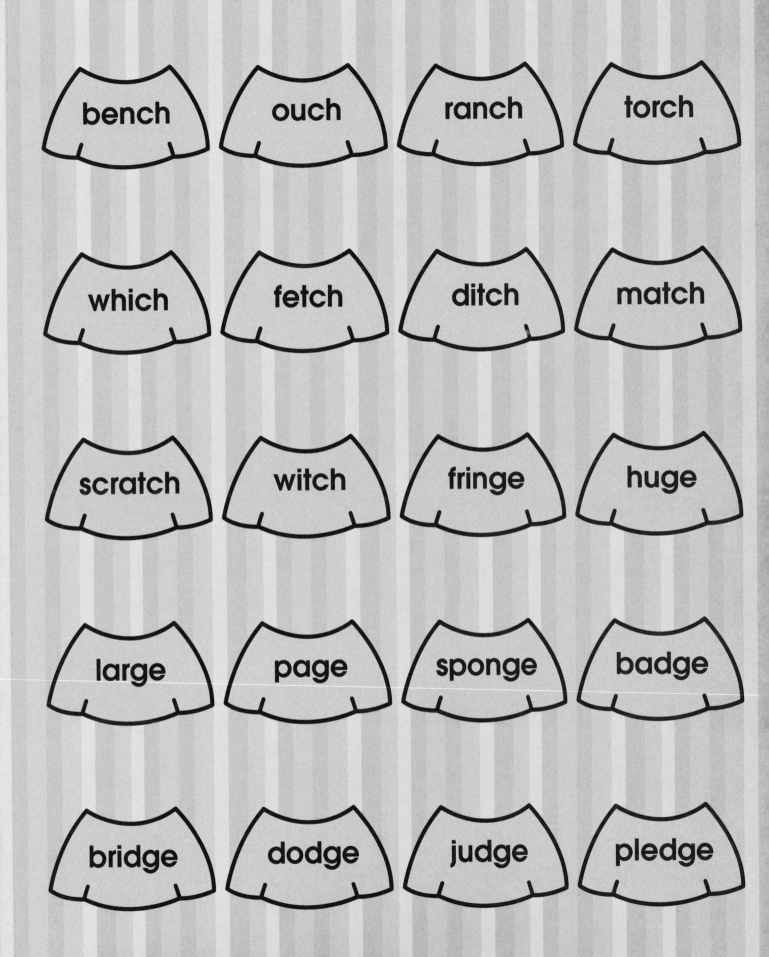

bench

ouch

ranch

torch

which

fetch

ditch

match

scratch

witch

fringe

huge

large

page

sponge

badge

bridge

dodge

judge

pledge

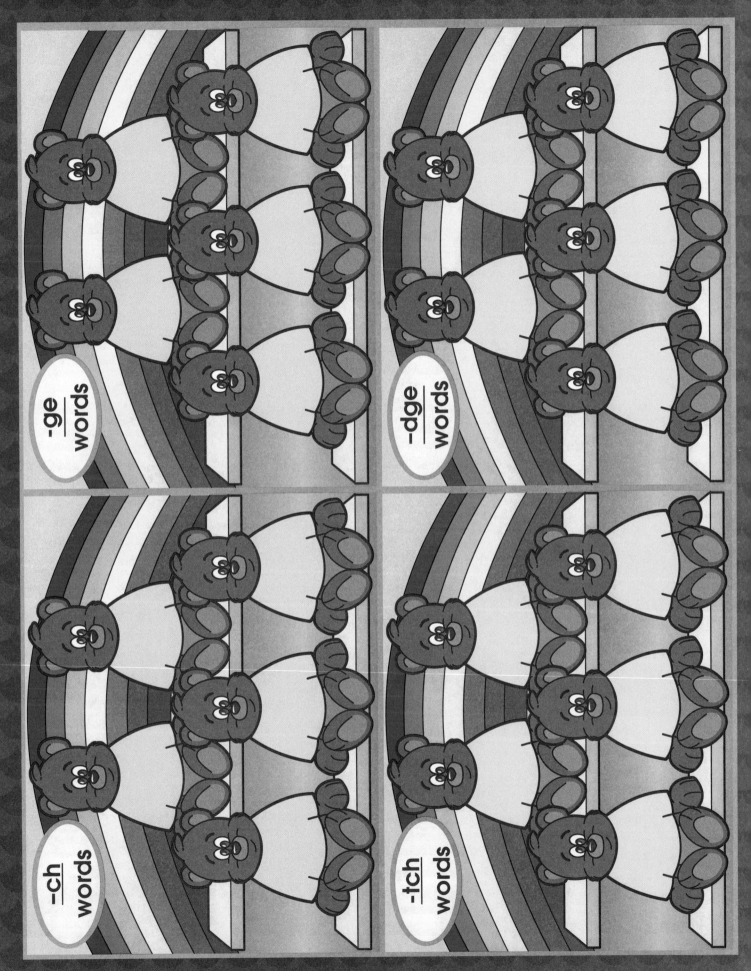

-ld words

gold

-nd words

round

bald	build	child	cold
could	gold	scald	should
wild	world	behind	blind
friend	round	ground	kind
pond	pretend	refund	sand

–nd words

–ld words

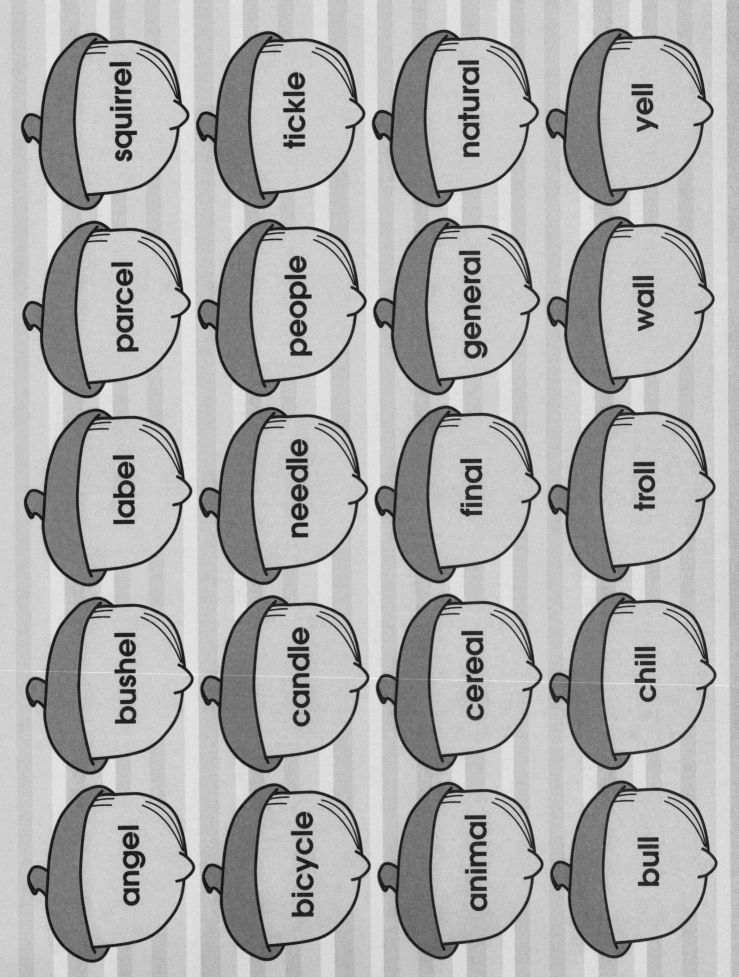

squirrel

tickle

natural

yell

parcel

people

general

wall

label

needle

final

troll

bushel

candle

cereal

chill

angel

bicycle

animal

bull

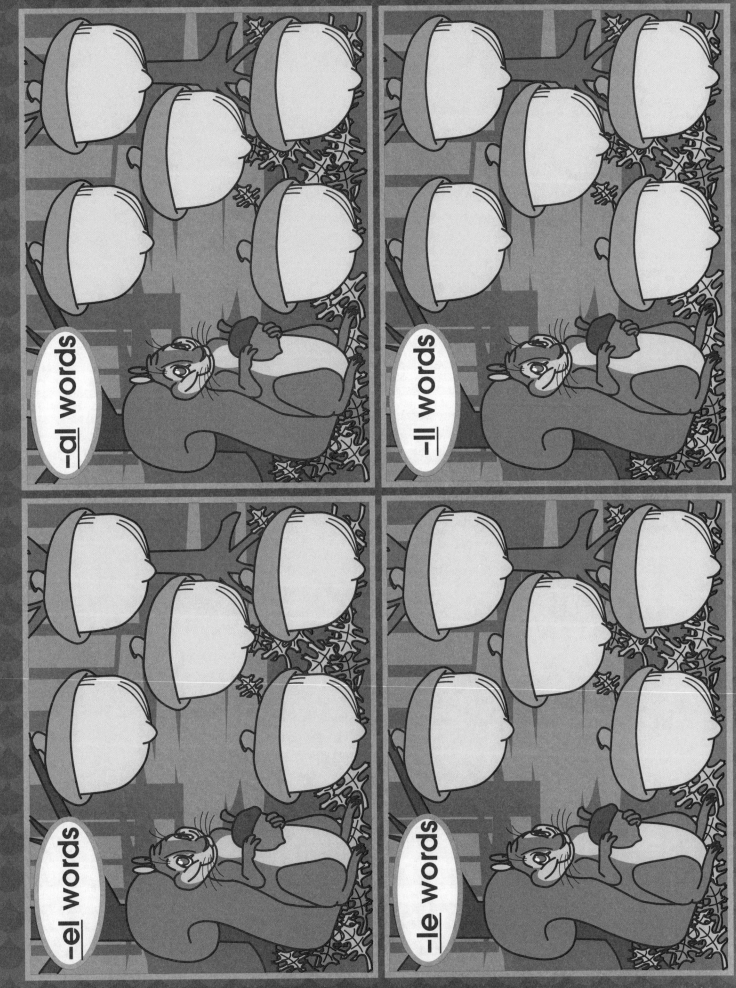

-al words

-ll words

-el words

-le words

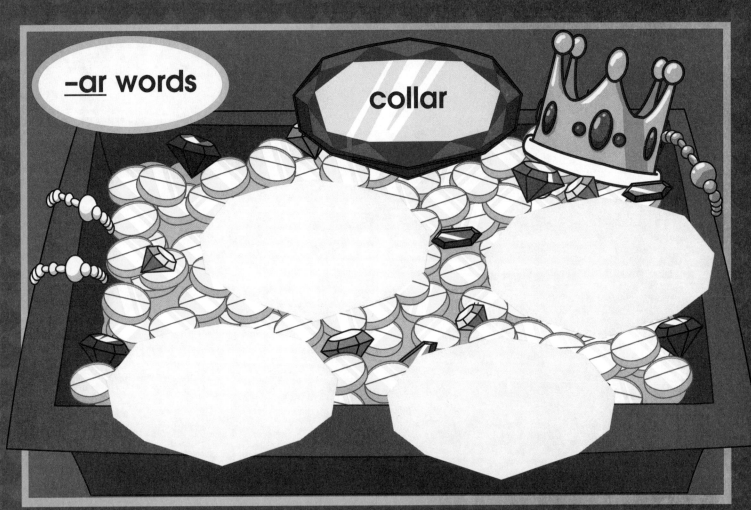

-ar words

collar

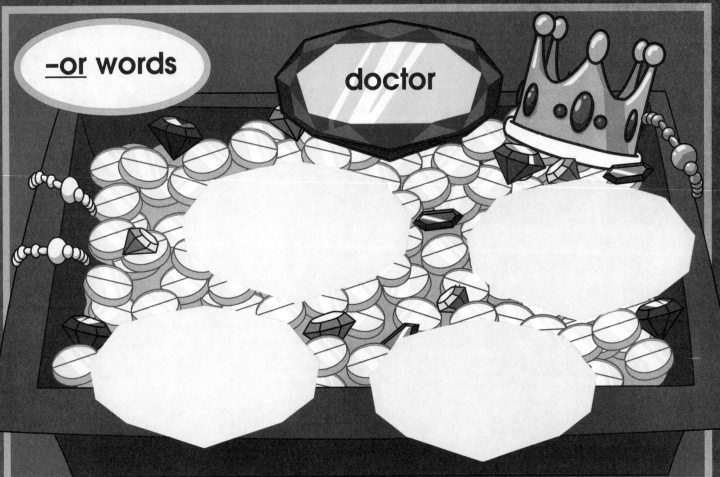

-or words

doctor

-er words

spider

-ure words

treasure

guitar

doctor

cover

future

treasure

dollar

color

barber

spider

picture

cedar

armor

harbor

number

nature

collar

scholar

favor

ginger

measure

34

-er
words

-ure
words

-ar
words

-or
words

-an, -ain, and -en words

human

-an

-an

-an

-ain

-ain

-ain

-ain

-en

-en

-en

-en

38

-eon, -on, and -in words

button

-on

-on

-on

-eon

-eon

-eon

-eon

-in

-in

-in

-in

40

human
slogan
urban
veteran
again
captain
fountain
mountain
dozen
oven
rotten
siren
chameleon
dungeon
pigeon
surgeon
button
cotton
dragon
lemon
begin
dolphin
robin
toxin

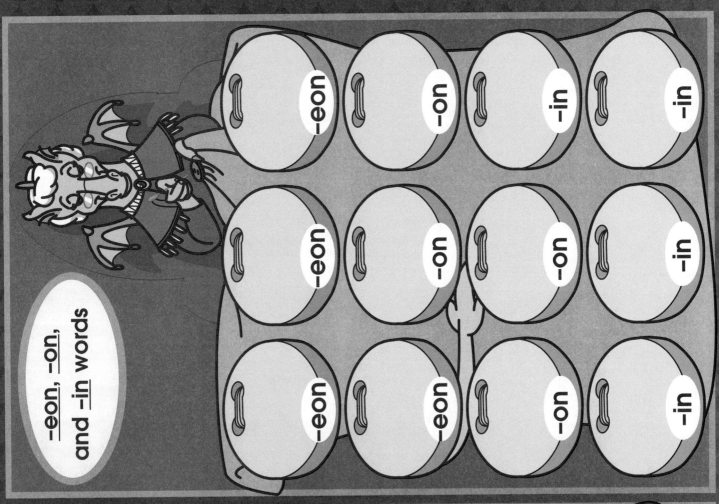

-eon, -on, and -in words

-eon -on -in -in

-eon -on -on -in

-eon -eon -on -in

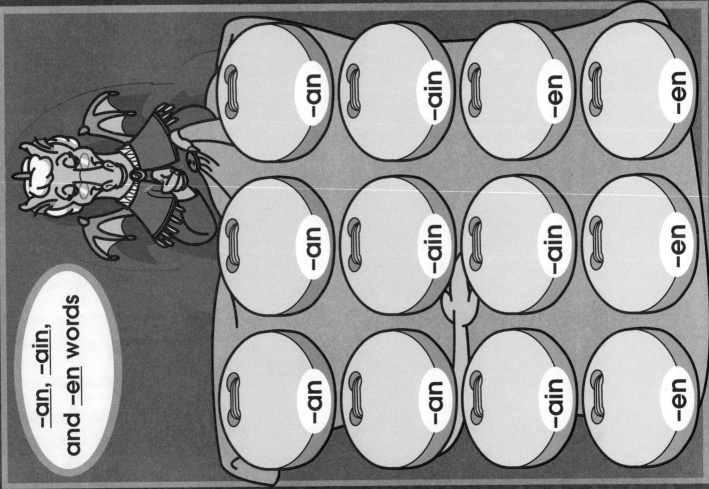

-an, -ain, and -en words

-an -ain -en -en

-an -ain -ain -en

-an -an -ain -en

knight knee knob knot

know need night no

not now wrap wring

wrist write wrong rack

read right ring rope

kn words

n words

wr words

r words

53

54

climb

-mb words

swim

-m words

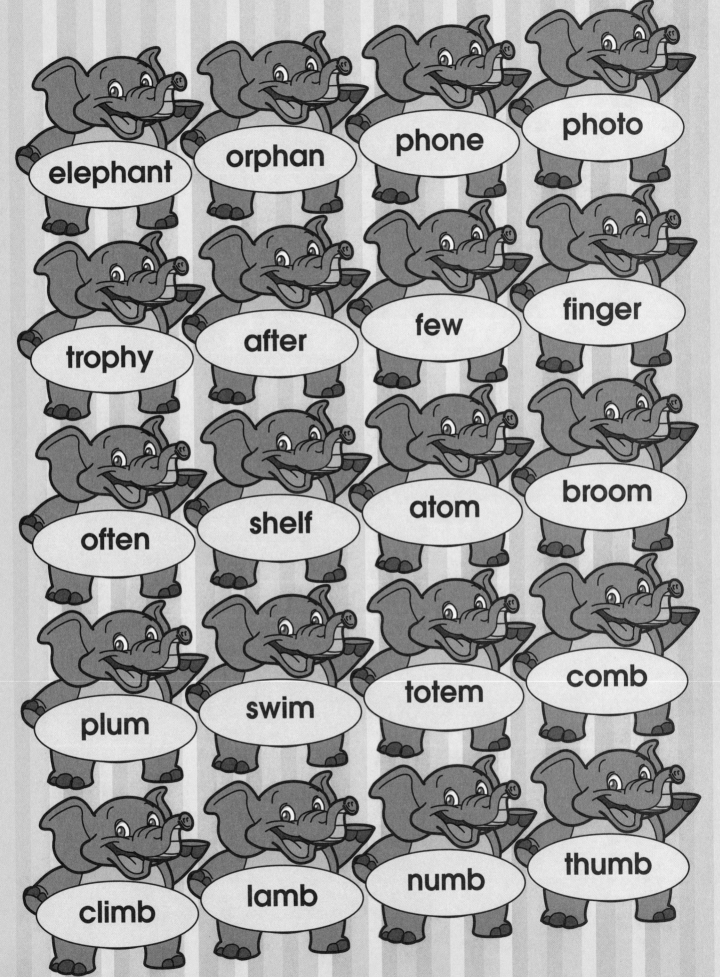

elephant

orphan

phone

photo

trophy

after

few

finger

often

shelf

atom

broom

plum

swim

totem

comb

climb

lamb

numb

thumb

ph words

f words

-mb words

-m words

silent b, g, and h words

g

sign
g

debt
b

hour
h

b

h

silent l, t, and w words

t

depot t

calf l

sword w

l

w

crumb
b

debt
b

doubt
b

limb
b

design
g

gnat
g

reign
g

sign
g

hour
h

herb
h

honor
h

heir
h

calf
l

half
l

salmon
l

would
l

castle
t

depot
t

fasten
t

listen
t

answer
w

sword
w

whole
w

wrinkle
w

silent **b**, **g**, and **h** words

silent **l**, **t**, and **w** words

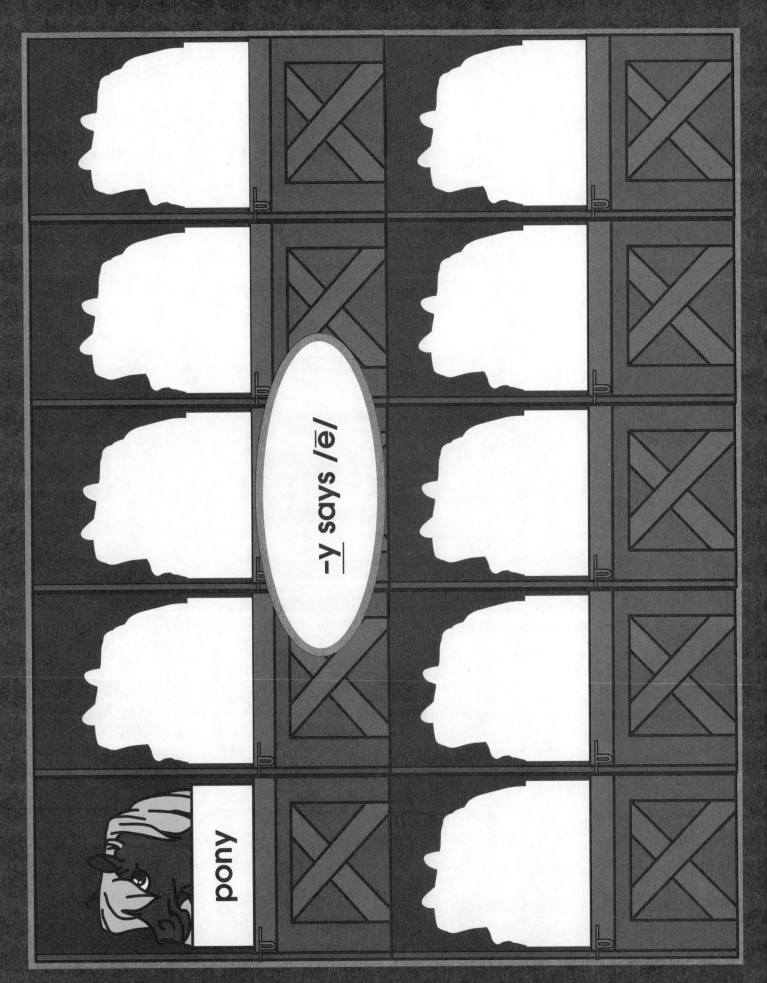

-y says /ē/

pony

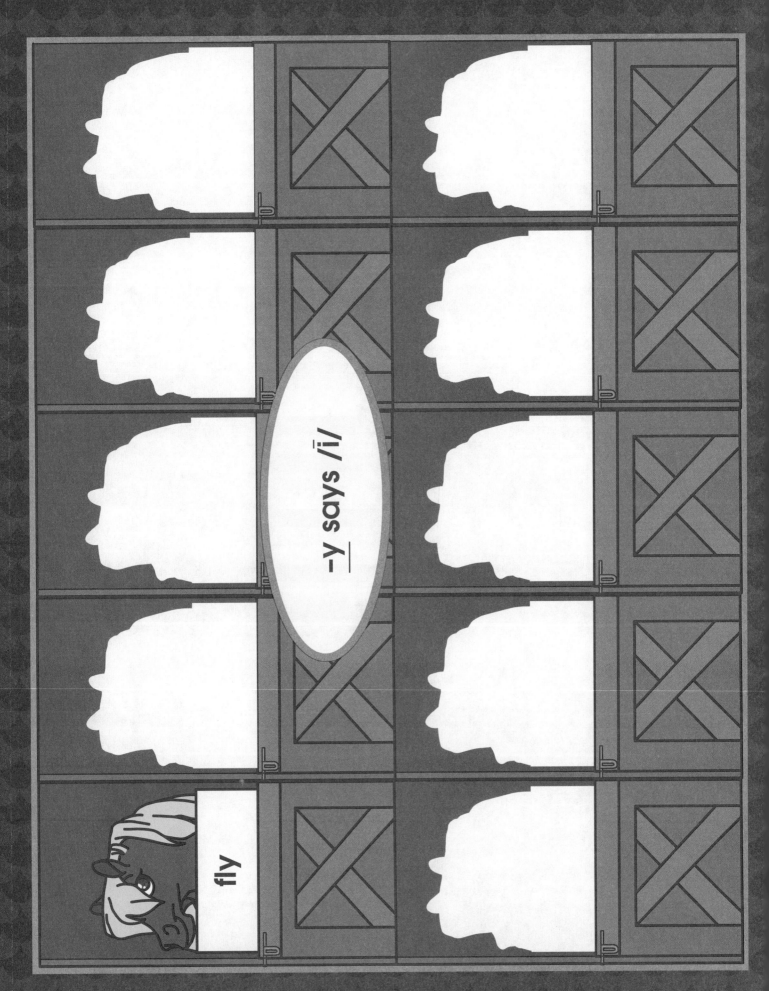

-y says /ī/

fly

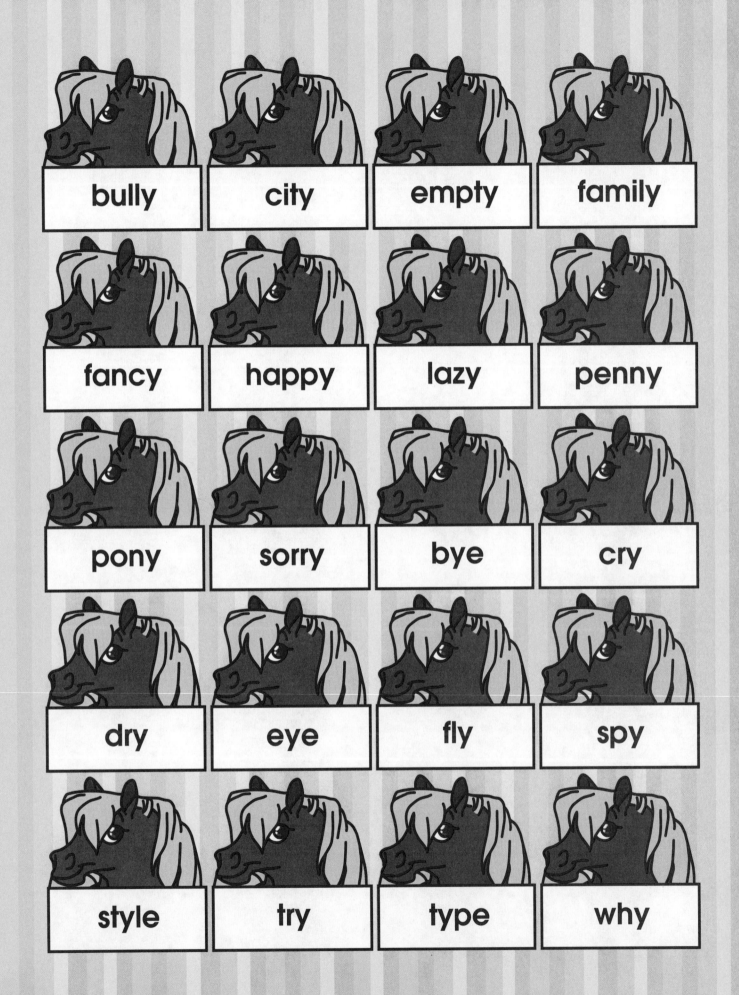

bully	city	empty	family
fancy	happy	lazy	penny
pony	sorry	bye	cry
dry	eye	fly	spy
style	try	type	why

-y says /ē/

-y says /ē/

-y says /ī/

-y says /ī/

apple

a̲ says /ă/

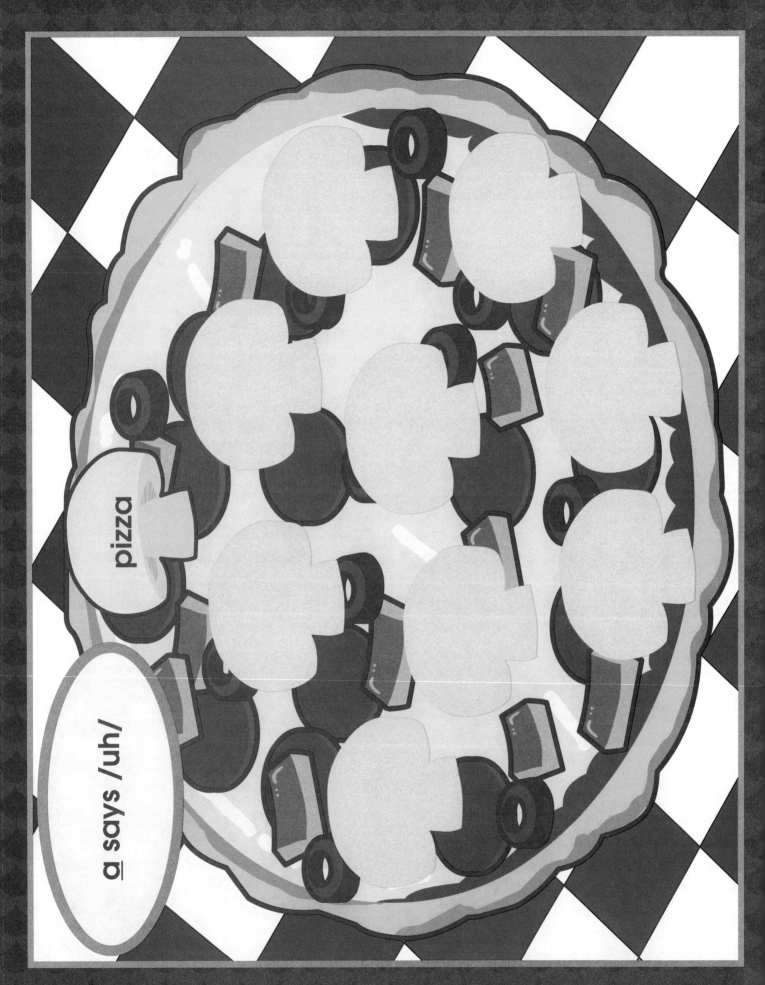

pizza

<u>a</u> says /uh/

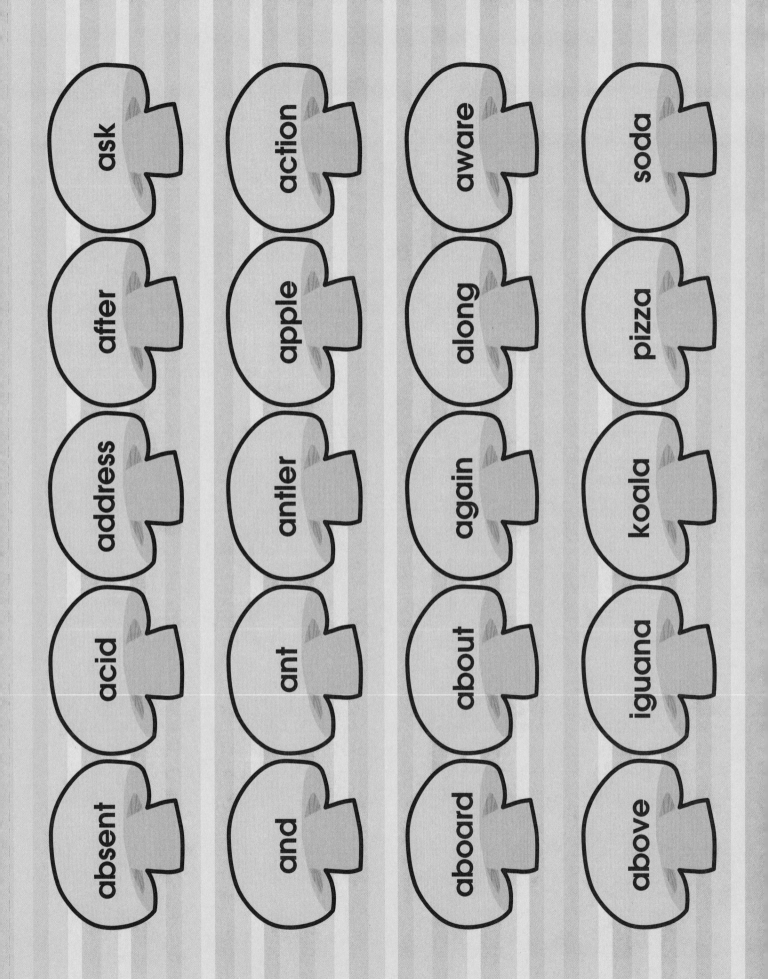

ask

after

address

acid

absent

action

apple

antler

ant

and

aware

along

again

about

aboard

soda

pizza

koala

iguana

above

a says /ă/

a says /uh/

sour

ou says /ow/

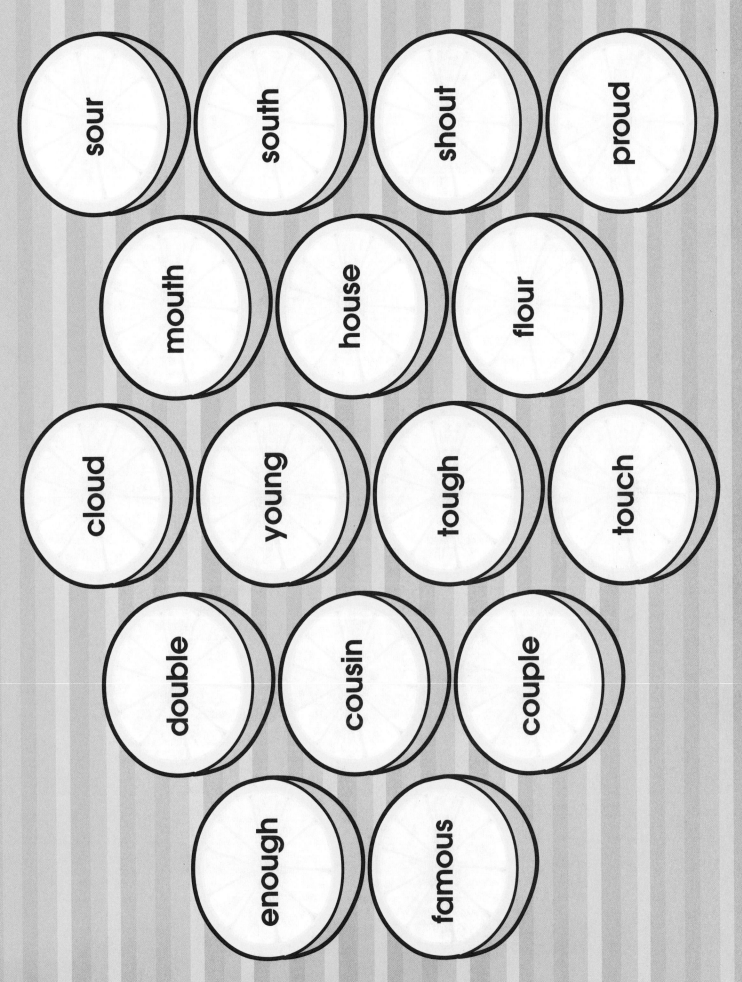

sour

south

shout

proud

mouth

house

flour

cloud

young

tough

touch

double

cousin

couple

enough

famous

91

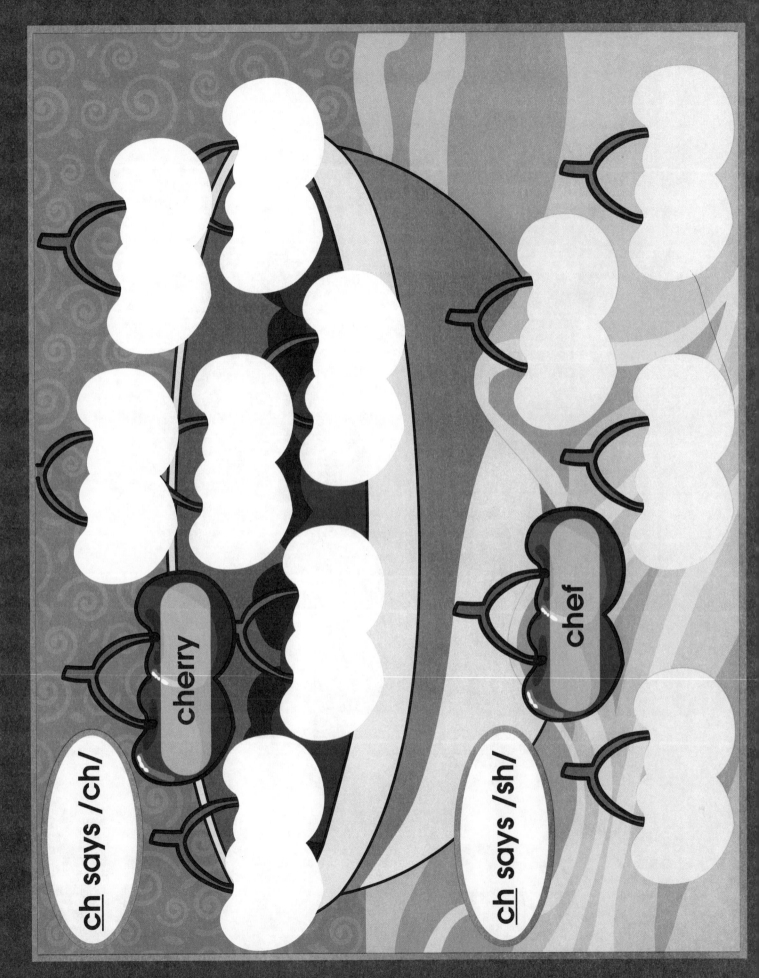

ch says /ch/

cherry

ch says /sh/

chef

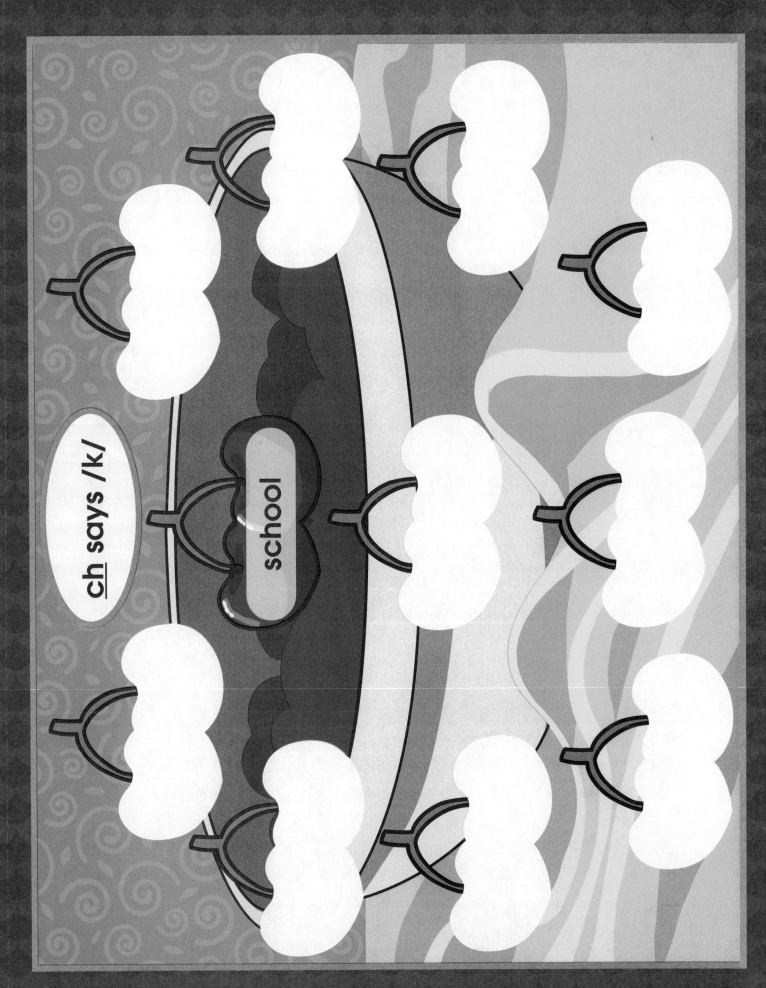

ch says /k/

school

chance	change	cherry
chicken	kitchen	much
orchard	pinch	charade
chef	chute	machine
parachute	ache	anchor
chord	chorus	chrome
echo	mechanic	orchid
scheme	school	stomach

 #3124 Full-Color Phonics Word Sorts

ch says /ch/

ch says /sh/

ch says /k/

ough says __/ew/__

ough says __/uff/__

ough says __/aw/__

ough
says /ow/

ough
says /off/

ough
says /ō/

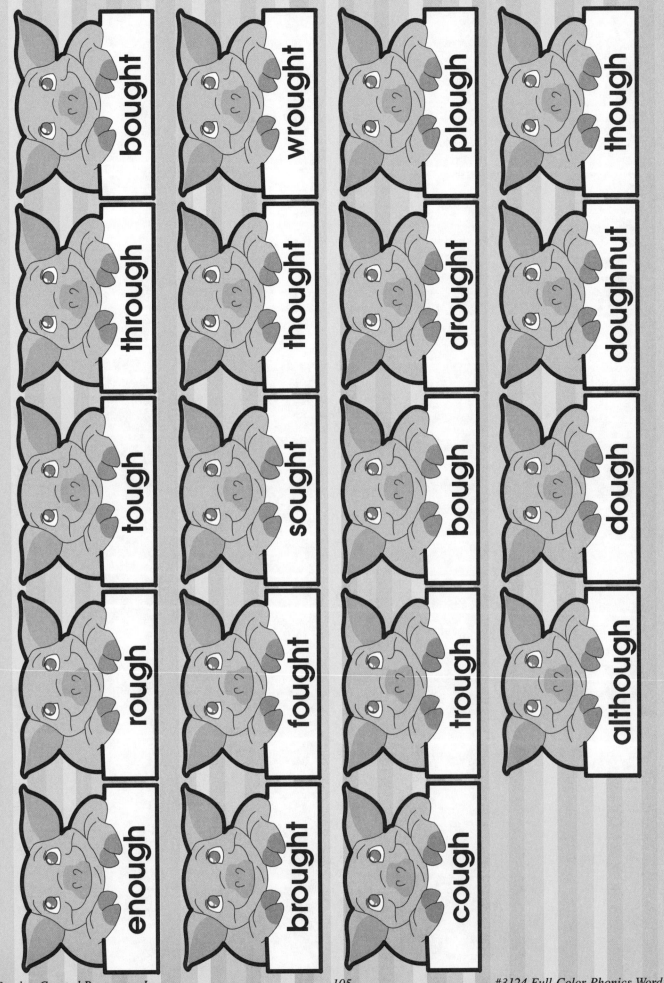

bought	wrought	plough	though
through	thought	drought	doughnut
tough	sought	bough	dough
rough	fought	trough	although
enough	brought	cough	

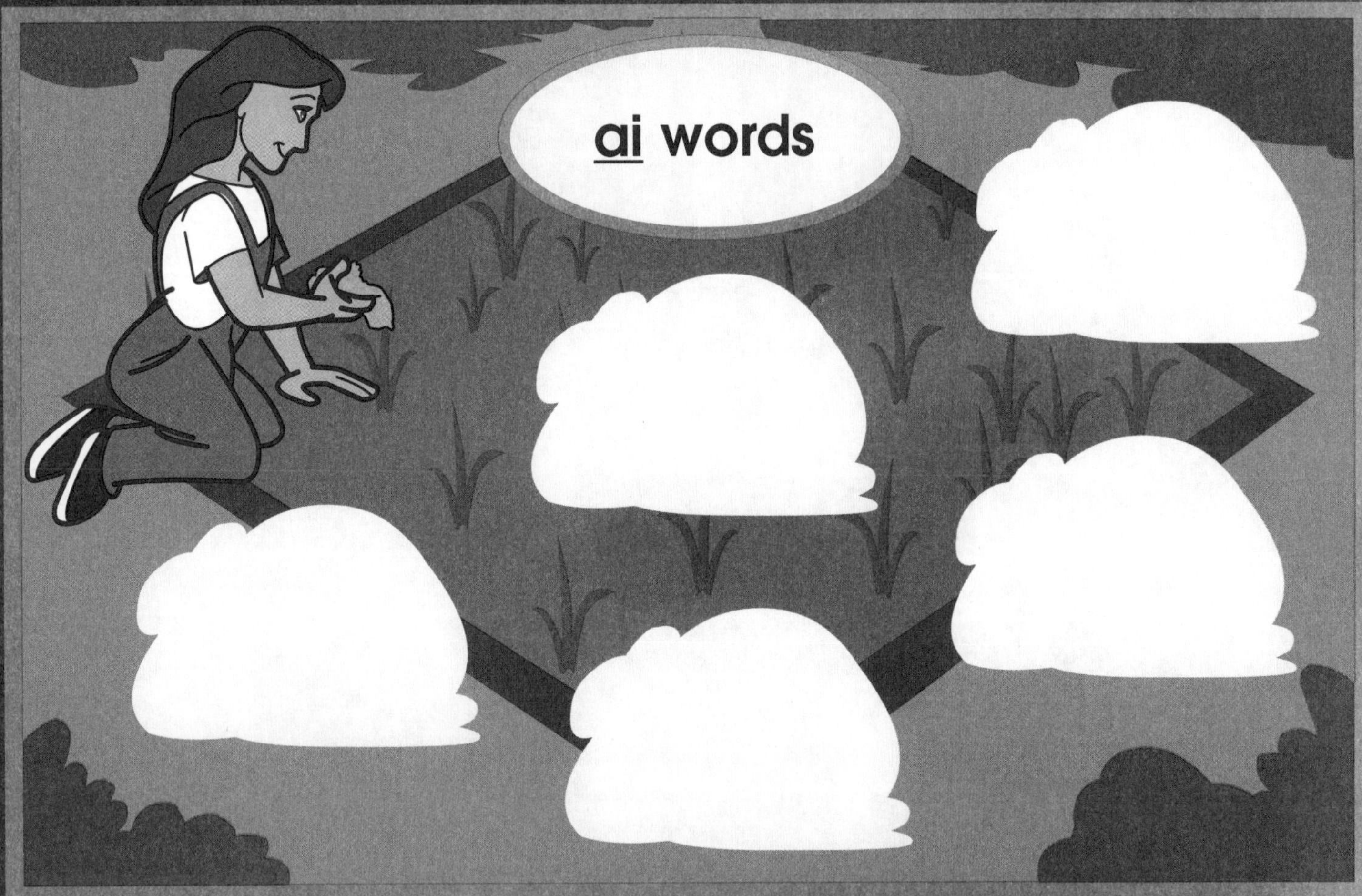
ai words

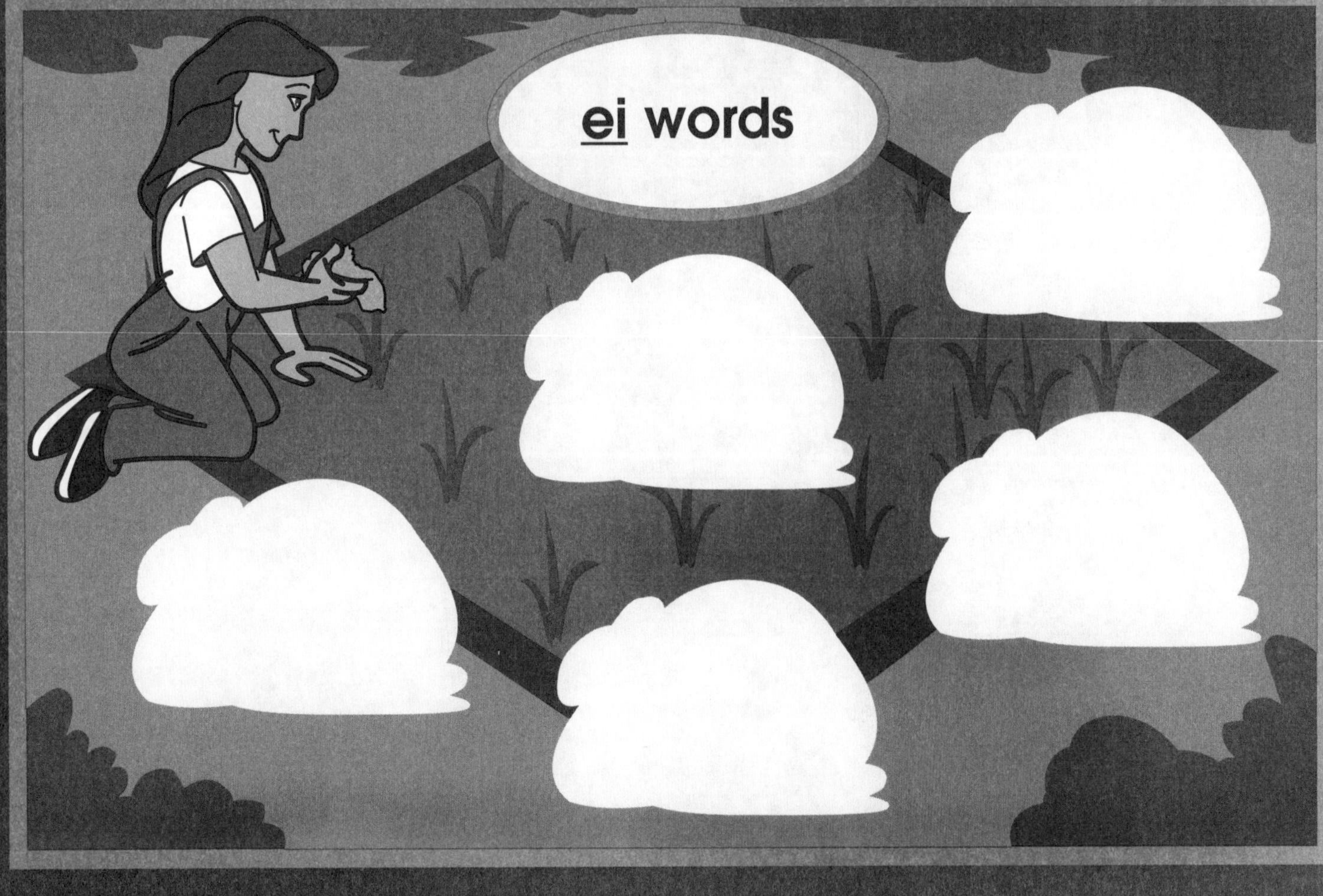
ei words

ay words

ea words

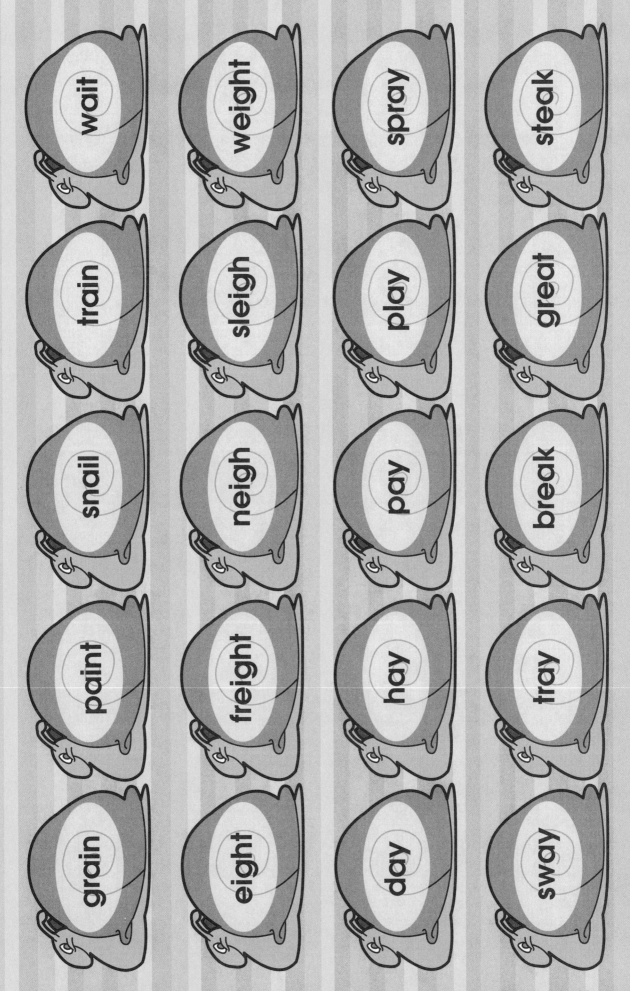

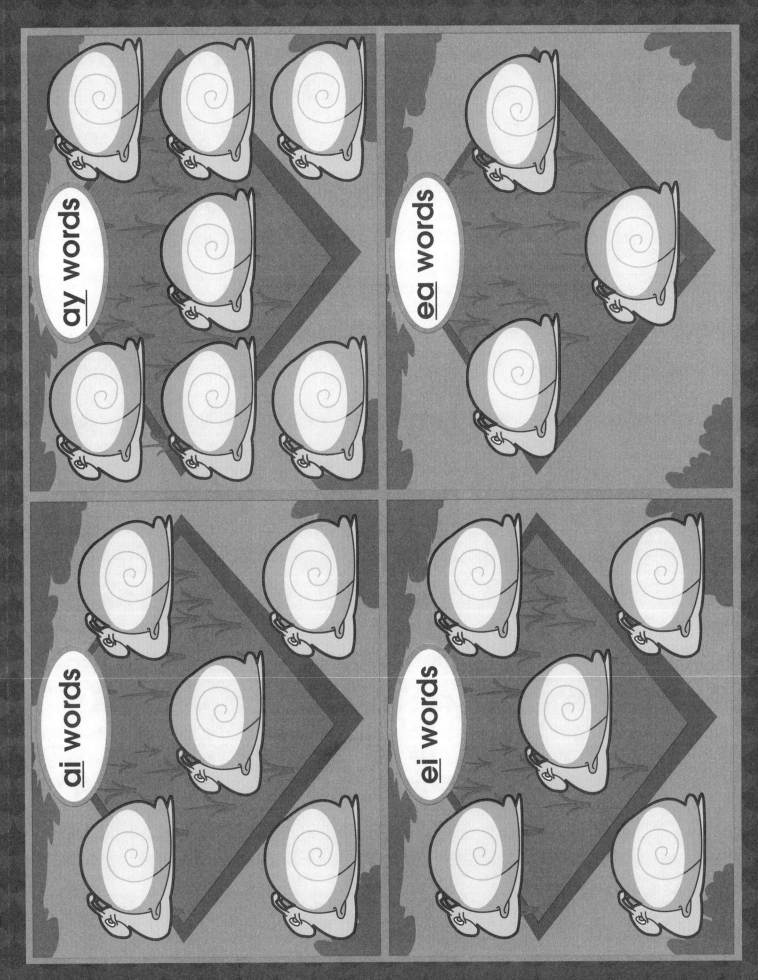

long e spelled ea, e, and ey

ea

ea

ea

e

e

e

ey

ey

ey

long e spelled ee, ie, and -y

ee

ee

ee

ie

ie

ie

-y

-y

-y

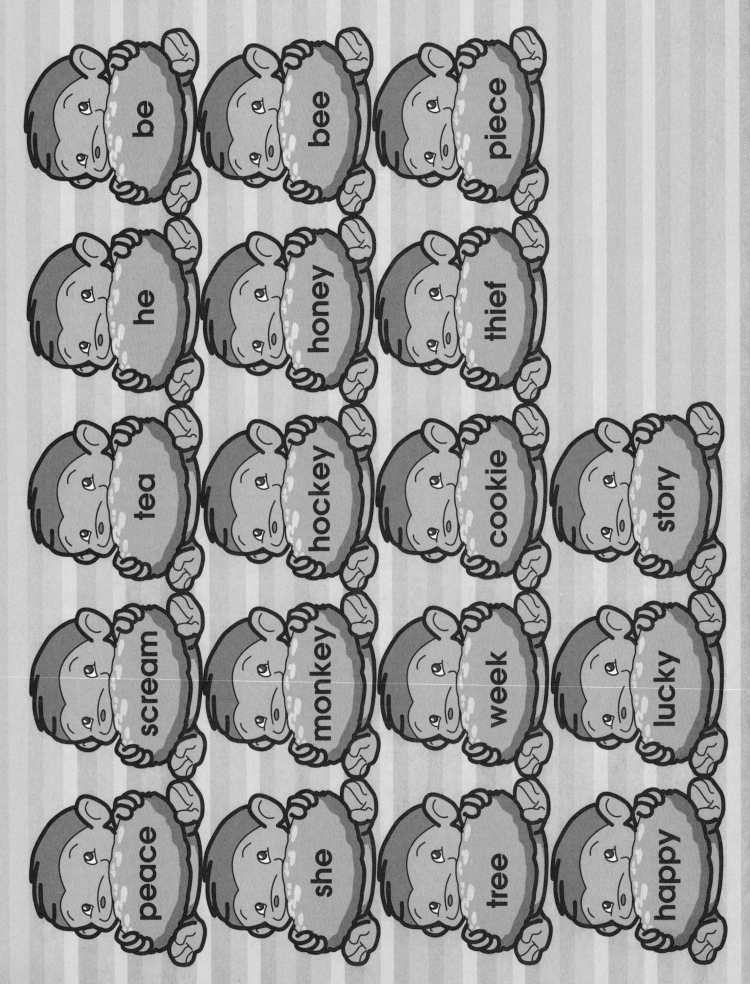

long e spelled
ee, ie, and -y

ee

ie

-y

ee

ie

-y

ee

ie

-y

long e spelled
ea, e, and ey

ea

e

ey

ea

e

ey

ea

e

ey

/air/ spelled
air, are, and ar

ar

ar

ar

ar

are

are

are

are

air

air

air

air

/air/ spelled
<u>arr</u>, <u>ear</u>, and <u>er</u>

er

er

er

er

ear

ear

ear

ear

arr

arr

arr

arr

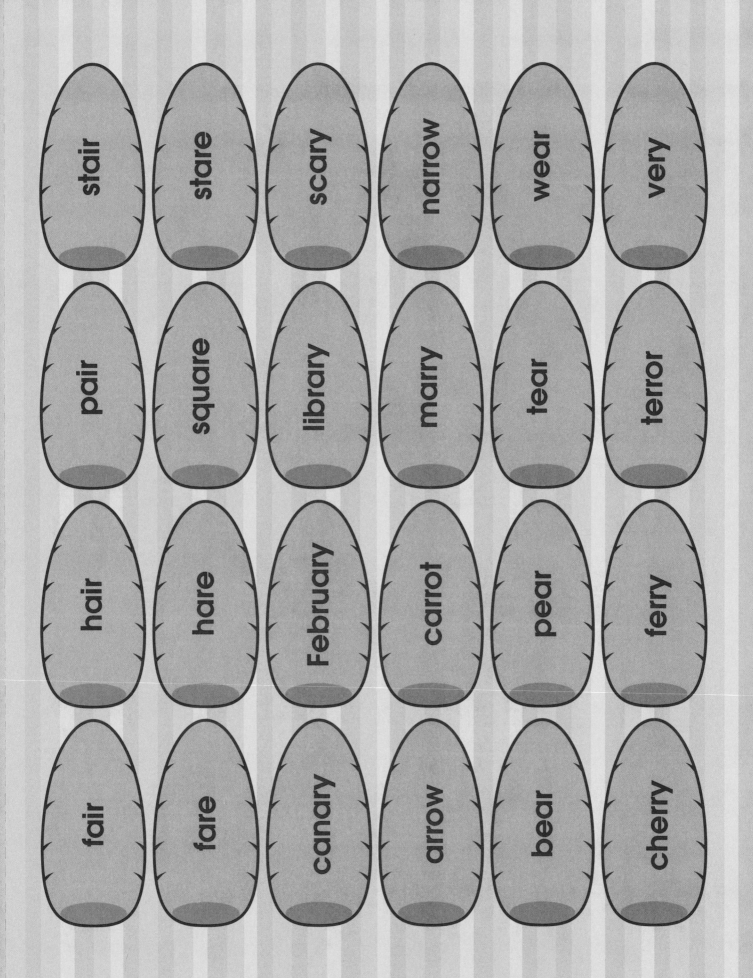

stair

stare

scary

narrow

wear

very

pair

square

library

marry

tear

terror

hair

hare

February

carrot

pear

ferry

fair

fare

canary

arrow

bear

cherry

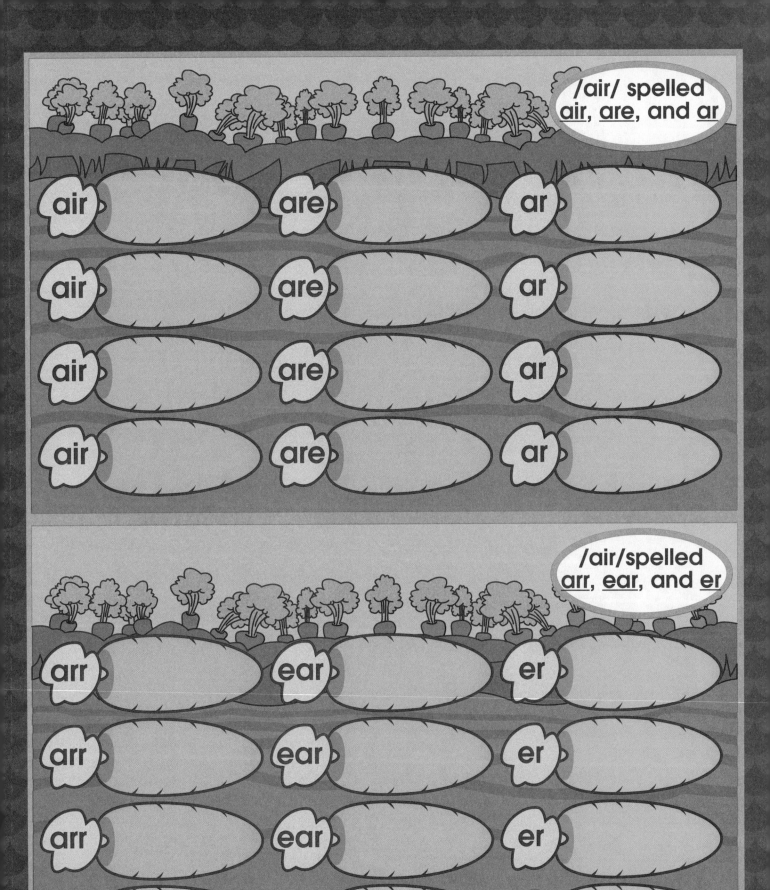

aw words

au words

al words

all words

awful

crawl

hawk

paws

yawn

caught

fault

haul

pause

sauce

chalk

false

malt

salt

walk

hall

small

stall

tall

wall

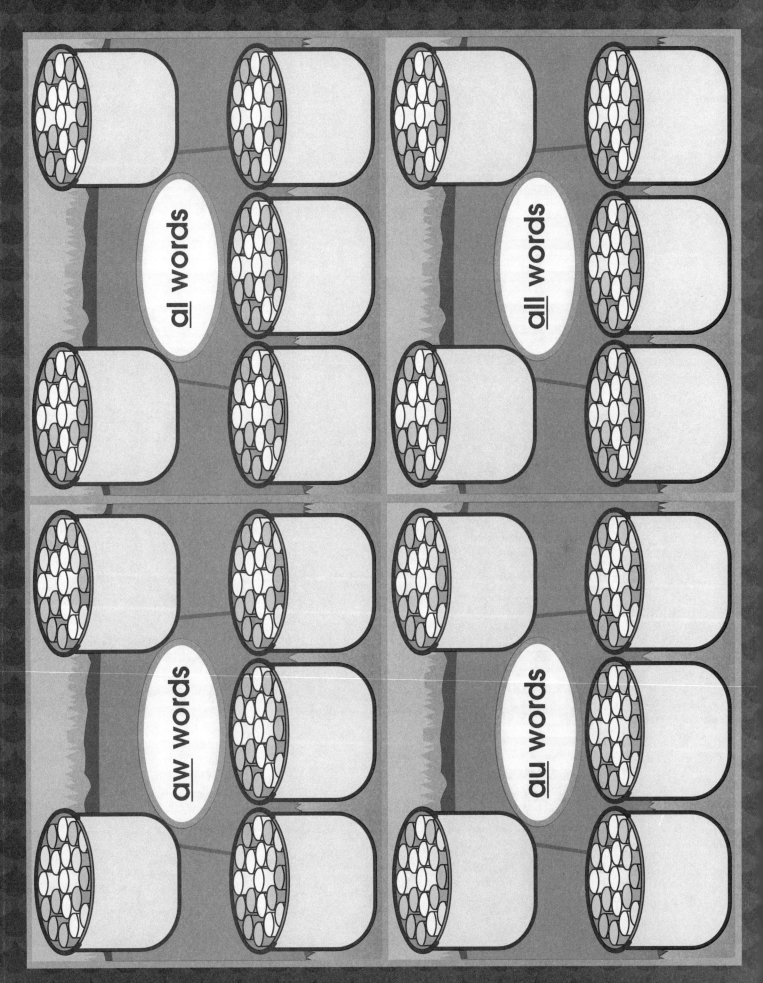

al words

all words

aw words

au words

ear words

eer words

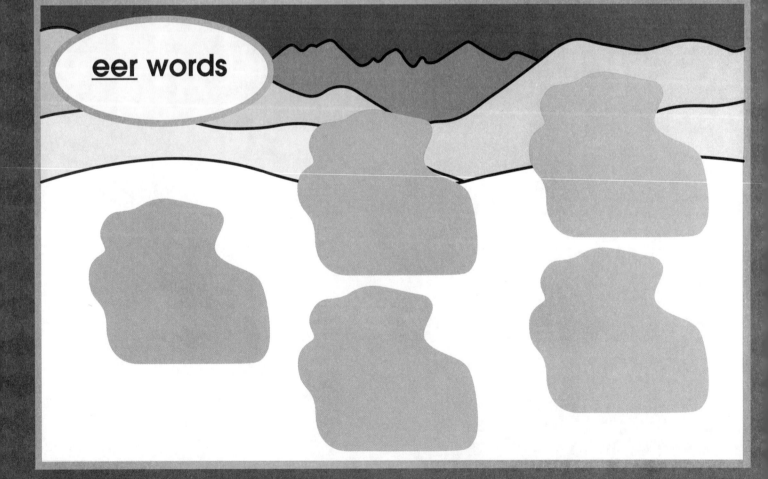

ere words

ier words

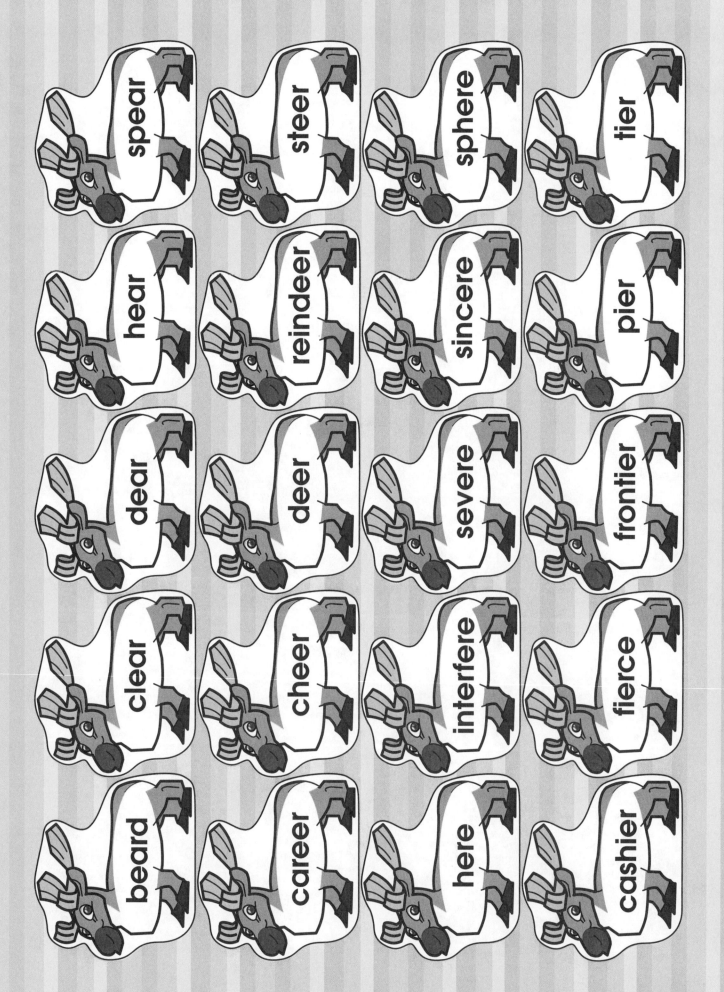

spear

steer

sphere

tier

hear

reindeer

sincere

pier

dear

deer

severe

frontier

clear

cheer

interfere

fierce

beard

career

here

cashier

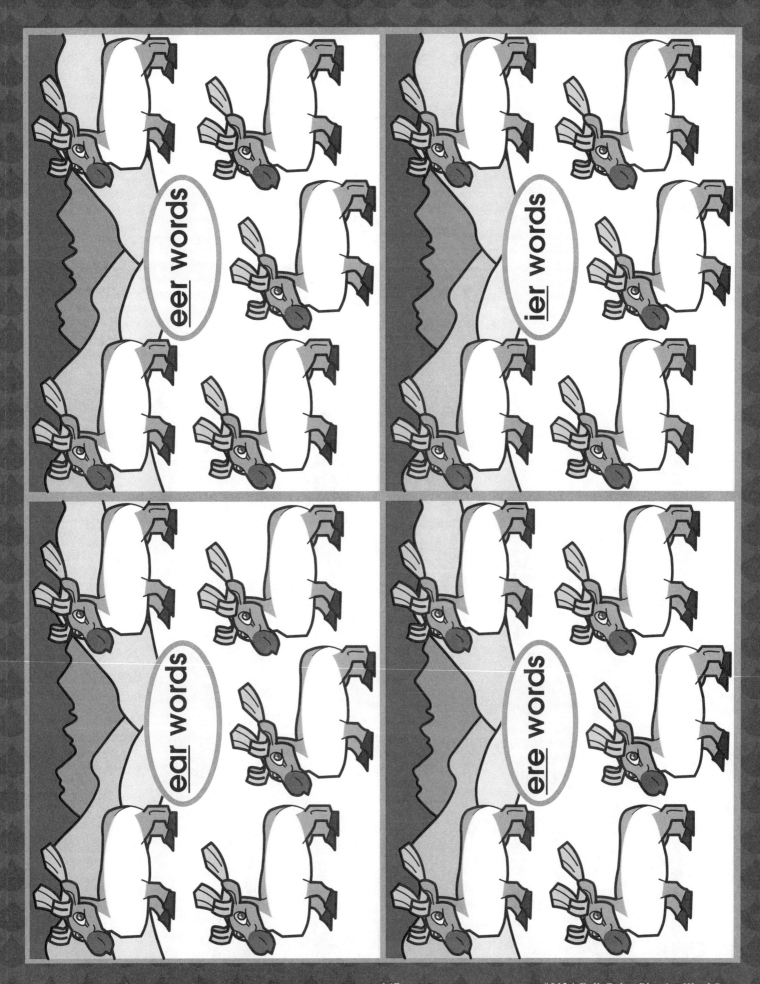

eer words

ier words

ear words

ere words

/or/ spelled
ar, oar, and oor

/or/ spelled
<u>or</u>, <u>ore</u>, and <u>our</u>

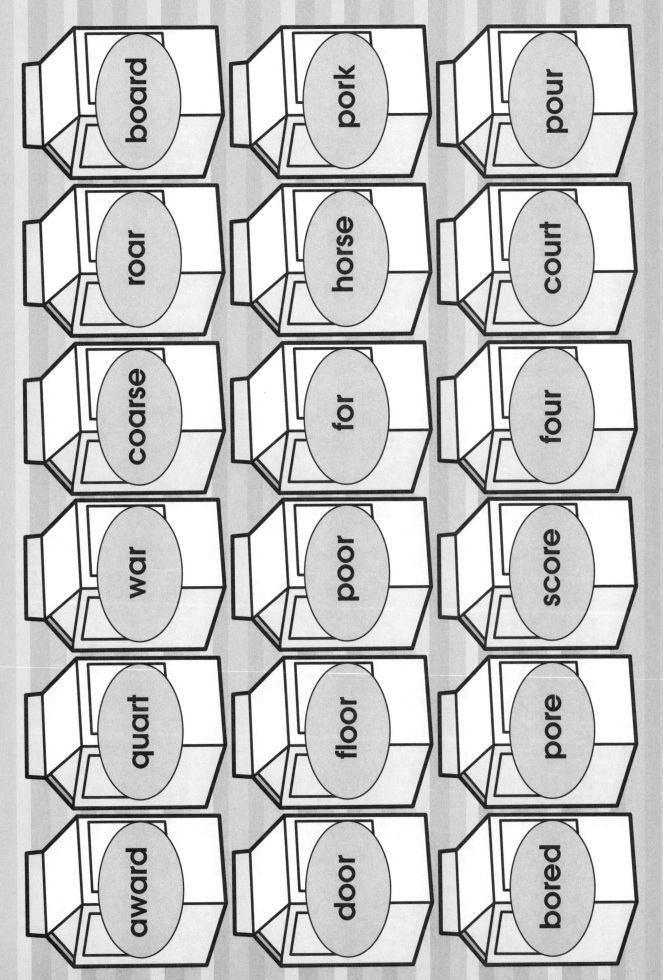

board

pork

pour

roar

horse

court

coarse

for

four

war

poor

score

quart

floor

pore

award

door

bored

or

or

or

ore

ore

ore

our

our

our

/or/ spelled or, ore, and our

ar

ar

ar

oar

oar

oar

oor

oor

oor

/or/ spelled ar, oar, and oor

/sh/ spelled <u>ci</u>

/sh/ spelled <u>si</u>

/sh/ spelled <u>ch</u>

/sh/ spelled <u>ssi</u>

#3124 Full-Color Phonics Word Sorts

/sh/ spelled **ti**

/sh/ spelled **xi**

/sh/ spelled **sh**

/sh/ spelled **ce**

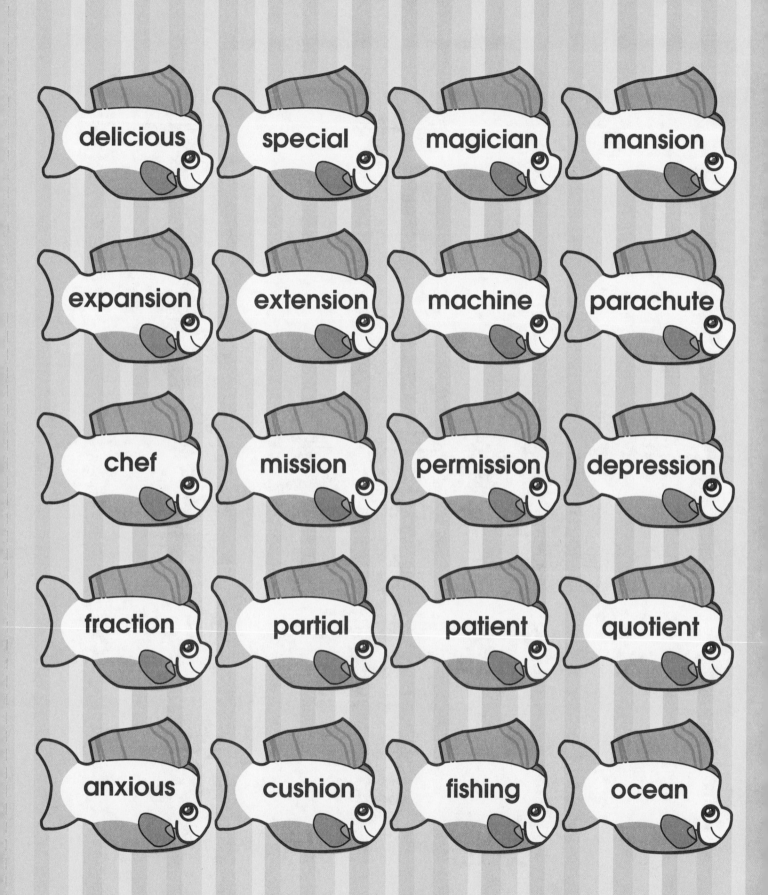

delicious

special

magician

mansion

expansion

extension

machine

parachute

chef

mission

permission

depression

fraction

partial

patient

quotient

anxious

cushion

fishing

ocean

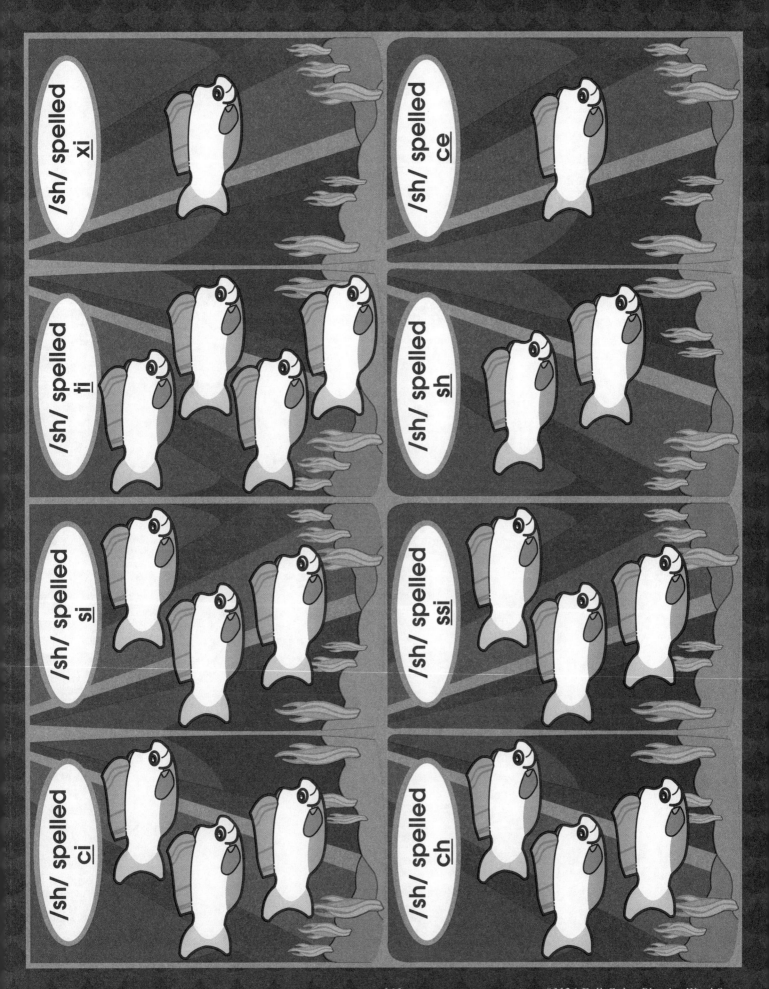

/sh/ spelled <u>xi</u>

/sh/ spelled <u>ce</u>

/sh/ spelled <u>ti</u>

/sh/ spelled <u>sh</u>

/sh/ spelled <u>si</u>

/sh/ spelled <u>ssi</u>

/sh/ spelled <u>ci</u>

/sh/ spelled <u>ch</u>

/ōō/ spelled o, oo, oe, and ove

oo

ove

oo

oo

ove

oo

oe

o

o

oe

o

/ōō/ spelled
ew, ue, ui, and u

ue

u

ui

ue

u

ue

ui

ew

ew

ew

ui

ew

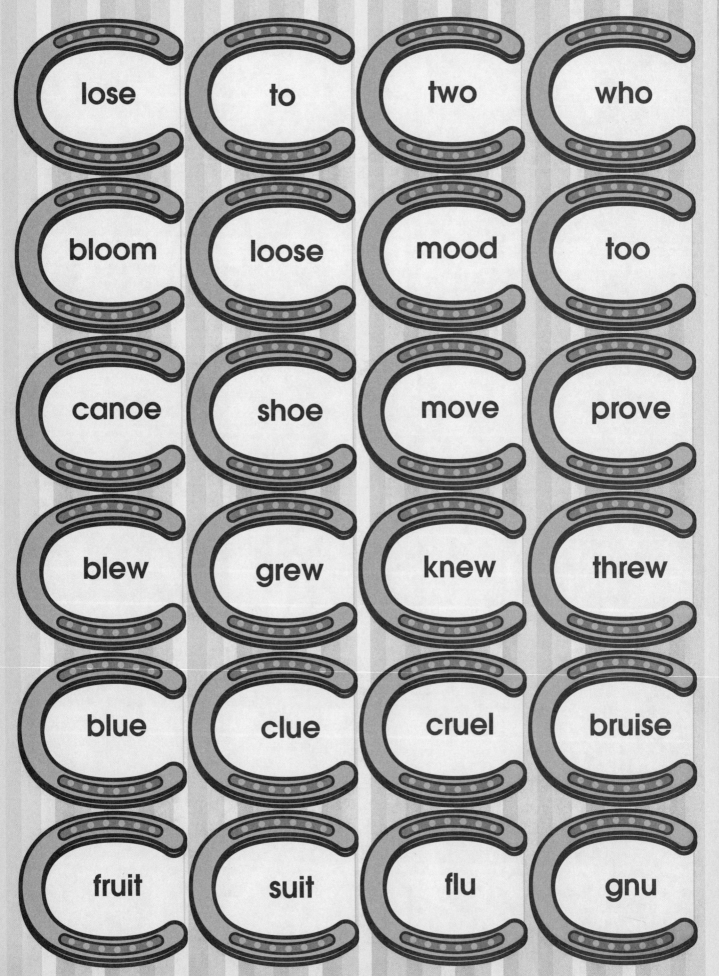

lose	to	two	who
bloom	loose	mood	too
canoe	shoe	move	prove
blew	grew	knew	threw
blue	clue	cruel	bruise
fruit	suit	flu	gnu

Go ahead 2 spaces.

JUPITER
You left your space suit on Mars. Go back and get it.

MERCURY
Oops! Wrong planet! Go to Venus.

Go again.

MARS

Trade places with another player.

PLUTO
FINISH

Go back 2 spaces.

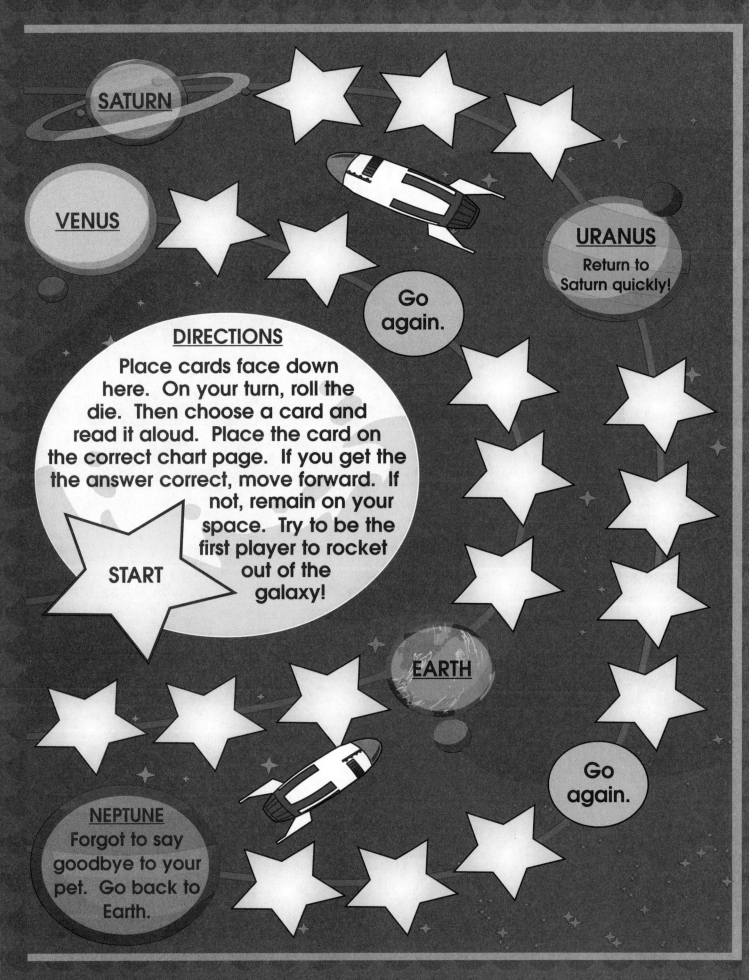

SATURN

VENUS

URANUS
Return to Saturn quickly!

Go again.

DIRECTIONS

Place cards face down here. On your turn, roll the die. Then choose a card and read it aloud. Place the card on the correct chart page. If you get the the answer correct, move forward. If not, remain on your space. Try to be the first player to rocket out of the galaxy!

START

EARTH

Go again.

NEPTUNE
Forgot to say goodbye to your pet. Go back to Earth.